"As our culture collapses around us, the issues of bioethics lie at the heart of its crisis. And why? Because they address the foundational questions of human nature, and every culture is premised on its own assumptions about what it means to be human.

"In this series these extraordinary questions are tackled with due seriousness (they make everyone think) and yet also with accessibility (no one who thinks will be excluded). It is hard to imagine a more important set of questions or a more timely publication."

Nigel M. de S. Cameron, Ph.D.
Provost, Trinity International University

"These booklets are packed with information and moral insights that will provide needed help to pastors, health care professionals, and teachers seeking direction in the ever-changing world of bioethics. Nothing less than human dignity hangs in the balance."

Francis J. Beckwith, Ph.D.
Associate Professor of Philosophy, Culture, and Law
Trinity Graduate School and Trinity Law School
Trinity International University

D0039534

The BioBasics Series provides insightful and practical answers to many of today's pressing bioethical questions. Advances in medical technology have resulted in longer and healthier lives, but they have also produced interventions and procedures that call for serious ethical evaluation. What we can do is not necessarily what we should do. This series is designed to instill in each reader an uncompromising respect for human life that will serve as a compass through a maze of challenging questions.

This series is a project of The Center for Bioethics and Human Dignity, an international organization located just north of Chicago, Illinois, in the United States of America. The Center endeavors to bring Christian perspectives to bear on today's many difficult bioethical challenges. It develops book, audio tape, and video tape series; presents numerous conferences in different parts of the world; and offers a variety of other printed and computer-based resources. Through its membership program, the Center provides world-wide resources on bioethical matters. Members receive the Center's international journal, *Ethics and Medicine,* the Center's newsletter, *Dignity,* the Center's *Update Letters,* special World Wide Web access, an Internet News Service and Discussion Forum, and discounts on most bioethics resources in print.

For more information on membership in the Center or its various resources, including present or future books in the BioBasics Series, contact the Center at:

The Center for Bioethics and Human Dignity
2065 Half Day Road
Bannockburn, IL 60015 USA
Phone: (847) 317-8180 Fax: (847) 317-8153
E-mail: cbhd@banninst.edu

Information and ordering is also available through the Center's World Wide Web site on the Internet: http://www.bioethix.org

BioBasics Series

Basic Questions on
End of Life Decisions

How Do We Know What's Right?

Gary P. Stewart, D.Min.
William R. Cutrer, M.D.
Timothy J. Demy, Th.D.
Dónal P. O'Mathúna, Ph.D.
Paige C. Cunningham, J.D.
John F. Kilner, Ph.D.
Linda K. Bevington, M. A.

kregel
PUBLICATIONS

Grand Rapids, MI 49501

Table of Contents

Termination of Life Support

Suffering

29. What is hospice, and what can it do for me or my loved one? **76**

Contributors

Linda K. Bevington, M.A., is the Project Manager for the Center for Bioethics and Human Dignity, Bannockburn, Illinois.

Paige C. Cunningham, J.D., has written numerous articles on abortion and the law; she is a coauthor of the amicus brief that Justice O'Connor cited in her discussion of viability in *Webster v. Reproductive Health Services.*

William R. Cutrer, M.D., served for many years as an obstetrician/gynecologist specializing in the treatment of infertility. He is currently serving as the Dallas/Fort Worth Area Director for The Christian Medical and Dental Society.

Timothy J. Demy, Th.M., Th.D., is a military chaplain and coauthor and author of numerous books and articles. He is a member of the Evangelical Theological Society.

John F. Kilner, Ph.D., is Director of the Center for Bioethics and Human Dignity, Bannockburn, Illinois. He is also Professor of Bioethics and Contemporary Culture at Trinity International University, Deerfield, Illinois.

Dónal P. O'Mathúna, Ph.D., is Associate Professor of Medical Ethics and Chemistry at Mount Carmel College of Nursing, Columbus, Ohio.

Gary P. Stewart, Th.M., D.Min., is a military chaplain and coauthor of numerous books and articles. He is a member of the Evangelical Theological Society.

Introduction

Life is the greatest gift a person possesses. Without it, nothing else would matter. There would be no one to love, nothing to become, nothing to accomplish. Nevertheless, with it there are disagreements, difficult decisions, and death. Life requires us to take the good with the bad, and end-of-life situations are no exception. The choices that each one of us makes throughout life are products of what we value. The value you place on life will determine the way you treat yourself and others throughout the end-of-life process. Please keep in mind, as you read and study this book, that these questions and answers deal with end-of-*life* issues, not death issues. The dying are not dead! They are alive with their dignity intact no matter what the debilitation. When you look into the face of a dying child, teenager, or adult, what do you see? Another patient, an invalid, a life not worth living, or one past his or her time? Do you see your fears, or would you rather not even look? Are you so focused on the *end* that you have lost sight of the *life?* Do you see someone to love; someone to care for, to touch, to hold, and to comfort? Do you see a human being, a person of worth equal to any other? How we answer these questions determines the way in which we will face life at its end.

This book is not intended to reproduce all the available information on the subject but rather to simplify, complement, and supplement other available sources that the reader is encouraged to consult. Some of these materials have been listed at the end of this book. This book is not intended to take the place of theological, legal, medical, or psychological counsel or treatment. If assistance in any of these areas is needed, please seek the services of a certified professional. The views expressed in this work are solely those of the authors and do not represent or reflect the position or endorsement of any governmental agency or department, military or otherwise.

1. Is death a natural part of life, and what should be my attitude toward it?

Many therapists suggest that death is a part of the human cycle of birth, death, and rebirth. They misleadingly imply that death is as natural as life and should, therefore, be readily accepted—each individual life ends in death and another individual is born to take his or her place.

Admittedly, death is natural in one sense: It is an event of the physical world that is to be expected. The word *natural* also refers to something that happens in the ordinary course of things, *without the intervention* of accident, violence, or disease.[1]

The Bible suggests, however, that humankind was brought into the world without the hint of death's being a part of the original creation event. God declared that his creation was "very good" (Gen. 1:31). Adam and Eve were introduced to the concept of death as something bad that would result if they chose to disobey God and eat from the tree of the knowledge of good and evil (Gen. 2:17). As long as they honored their relationship with the Lord, human death would not occur, nor would humanity experience guilt or shame (cf. Gen. 2:25). However, they succumbed to the temptation to be as great as the Creator and disobeyed the Lord, severing their relationship with Him.

The result was guilt, shame (Gen. 3:6–7), previously unknown physical pain, toil, and ultimately spiritual and physical death (Gen. 3:16–19). They were separated from God and, eventually, would experience

11

separation of the soul from the body. Death may be common, but it is not natural.

Death is an invasive intrusion into the natural order. Death is no more natural than an unwanted clot that develops in an artery. It is an evil that separates loved ones from one another. It creates anxiety, a deep sense of expected, and then realized, loss and grief.[2] It is an experience against which humanity has long fought and still tries to delay. Instinctively, we know that death is not natural. In fact, Scripture describes death as an enemy, the last enemy to be conquered as a result of the death, burial, and resurrection of Jesus Christ (1 Cor. 15:1–26).

Death is so unnatural that God sent His only Son as a remedy, to experience spiritual and physical death in the place of each human being and resurrection as the hope of eternal life with God for all who believe in Him. We must not view death as natural or as a friend that ends all suffering, for to do so would cause many to pursue death naïvely, falsely assuming that suffering cannot continue beyond death (Luke 16:19–31; 2 Cor. 5:10) and bypassing the valuable lessons of life and love that God has for us and those around us during the dying process. It is because of disobedience, i.e., sin, that humanity must endure suffering as life approaches the reality of death.

Yet, at the same time, we must remember that death is a *defeated* enemy. We should not fear it. We should not desperately resist it. God allows it in his mercy so that we need not suffer forever or spend an eternity burdened by the fallenness of the world. As we are to receive life humbly as a gift, so too we can accept death humbly when it comes. We must recognize that our efforts to do battle with the enemy will necessarily one day prove futile; yet we must also trust that the One who has defeated death can grant us new life as well.

When we think of our own mortality and our eventual death, we must do so with an eye to the way we live. Our professional or occupational successes or failures, important as these may be do not matter. Do we genuinely live so that we can be loved, and do we love so that others can live genuinely? Do we let others care for us, and do we care for others, those whom we have known in their infancy, youth, adulthood, and those, at any age, with whom we have walked into the valley of death? The dying process and death are the enemy, not those who experience them. Until we have learned to love, especially those who are the weakest among us, dying will remain a terminally threatening and isolating process, and death an appropriately desired end. Being loved and loving others, especially Christ, gives us a sense of fulfillment that brings a satisfying sense of completion: It provides us with a willingness to let go of this life to embrace the next with anticipation.

2. *When am I dying or in the "dying process"?*

One could say that we are all dying—that aging itself is a terminal disease—for eventually it takes us if nothing else does beforehand. However, it is not wise to casually refer to life as terminal just because we will all one day experience death's intrusion. Thinking of life as a terminal arrangement that begins at birth robs life of its potential and beauty. It also makes discussions about end-of-life treatment confusing. Medical technology has advanced to the point that we must limit the use of the word *terminal* to a particular period of life often called the *dying process*.

The most important thing to be said about the dying process is that it is a part of the *living process* (see Figure 2–1). Dying is part of living because the dying are still living. Accordingly, dying people must be accorded the same respect and protections that are due all living human beings created in the image of God.

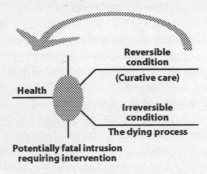

Figure 2–1: The Living Process

When healthy people suffer a potentially fatal illness or injury (anywhere from a cut to cancer), the impaired condition that results can either be reversible or irreversible. Calling it *reversible* means there is a medical intervention that can remove the threat to life and can restore or generally improve one's health. If such medical intervention does not exist, then the condition is *irreversible,* i.e., *terminal:* The impaired condition will eventually cause death. Such persons are *dying,* i.e., are in the *dying process* (see Figure 2–2).

Various categories are helpful for understanding and responding to the predicament of people in the dying process. The categories may reflect how badly people

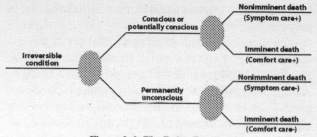

Figure 2–2: The Dying Process

are impaired, or how near their death is. For example, people may be so seriously impaired that they are *permanently unconscious*. They have lost their ability to interact with the world in any way—giving or receiving communication—and that ability cannot be restored. Those who do not fall into this category are either *conscious* or *potentially conscious*. Other categories reflect nearness to death. For example, those for whom death is *imminent* will die soon (in a few hours, days, weeks, or at most, months) no matter what medical interventions are attempted, whereas others will not. Although the category sounds a little vague, it is precise enough to have long served as a legal and not just as a moral category.[3] It cannot be more precise than this simply because people whose bodily systems are failing and who are clearly dying "soon" may sometimes unpredictably linger longer than expected.

3. How aggressively should we treat people with potentially fatal illnesses or injuries?

In an important sense, we should treat all living human beings aggressively. Although the medical intervention may change, we should always aggressively care for each patient. The primary form this care

15

takes—curative care, symptom care, comfort care, or respect care—will vary depending on the patient's condition (see Figure 2–2). People with reversible conditions, out of respect for life, should elect to use all necessary medical intervention to restore them to health. This is *curative care* (see Figure 2–1). Some patients, however, have fatal infections, injuries, or diseases that cannot be reversed through medical intervention. These people have entered the dying process—their condition is terminal. Since curative care is not possible, other forms of care are required.

Most patients with an irreversible condition are conscious or potentially conscious, i.e., they have the potential to regain consciousness at some time in the future. Many in this category are *not imminently dying* (see question 2). In such cases, though the underlying condition cannot be reversed, a large number of related medical problems typically develop over time—e.g., breathing difficulty, dehydration, kidney failure, or infection. These problems can be treated in a variety of ways. This is *symptom care*. Such care is often necessary not only for the sake of comfort but to support the life of the patient. Out of respect for life, patients and their caregivers will opt for all necessary symptom care.

When the condition of such patients deteriorates, however, and *death becomes imminent,* then patients or those empowered to make medical decisions for them (see question 13) are under no moral obligation to continue symptom care. Forgoing symptom care in this situation need not involve abandoning life or intending death. Rather, it can be an appropriate and humble response to an unavoidable reality: Death will come soon no matter what is done. Continued symptom care may even add a greater burden to the dying process through increased discomfort or by making communication with loved ones more difficult. Patients may reject such treatment when the burden outweighs the benefit. Sometimes, however, patients have special reasons for prolonging life to the last possible moment, such as the marriage of a child or the birth of a grandchild. Continued symptom care is appropriate under such circumstances. While imminently dying patients will usually stop symptom care at some point, we should do everything possible to ensure that they receive whatever treatments and medication that are necessary to relieve their discomfort. This is *comfort care*.

What about the other category of patients whose conditions are irreversible, i.e., those who are *permanently unconscious?* When their death becomes imminent, there will rarely be a reason to continue symptom care. Because, by definition, they are no longer able to interact with the world around them, they will not experience the benefits of a prolonged dying process in the special cases noted earlier (a child's marriage, and so forth). Admittedly, there may be such cases in which people other than the patient would benefit by prolonging the patient's dying process. But such interests should prevail only if there is evidence that the patient would support this prolongation. Patients should not be "used" unwillingly simply for another's benefit. Even comfort care is not needed by permanently unconscious patients in the same way that conscious patients need it because permanently unconscious patients do not experience conscious discomfort (comatose patients who may experience pain are by definition not permanently unconscious). It is still appropriate, though, out of respect for them and their bodies, to provide whatever care can limit the visible deterioration of their bodies (e.g., keeping the mouth moist and clean, washing the body, and so forth). This is *respect care*. Respect care should be provided for all patients, no matter what their condition.

Perhaps the most perplexing category of patients are those who are *permanently unconscious* but *not imminently dying*. For example, patients in a so-called persistent vegetative state (PVS)—if the certainty and permanence of their condition can be established— are in this category. Among many things that are true of such patients, two are worth emphasizing here. First, there is a real danger that those said to be in a vegetative state will be viewed as "vegetables" and, therefore, somehow subhuman. Perhaps unintentionally they may be treated with less respect than they should receive. It may be wise to avoid using the terms *vegetable* or *vegetative* in order to safeguard against such loss of respect.

Second, people understandably struggle as they try to locate such patients on the continuum from life in this world to life in the next. When does a Christian, for example, move beyond interaction with this world to interaction with the spiritual realm beyond? Experientially, permanently unconscious patients have left this world, so the benefit *to the patients* of continued symptom care that merely keeps the bodily functions from ceasing is far from clear. They have either already begun their conscious, eternal interaction with the "world beyond this world," or they are being prevented from it—held in some sort of experiential limbo between the worlds. So, it is understandable if patients, or those empowered to make medical decisions for them, decide against symptom care in such circumstances and elect respect care only. They should not be hindered from doing so. However, since such patients are still alive by commonly accepted criteria, it is also ethically appropriate for permanently unconscious patients to receive the same symptom care given to all other terminal patients who are not imminently dying. Such symptom care can also be elected out of respect for human life. This decision, like the decision to decline symptom care, should be made in good conscience before God by the person(s) responsible.

We can summarize, then, how aggressively we should treat people with potentially fatal illnesses or injuries as follows. We must aggressively care for every patient, but the range of that care will differ depending on the condition of the patient. When curative care is appropriate, symptom care, comfort care, and respect care should also be provided. When curative care is not possible but symptom care is appropriate, comfort care and respect care are appropriate as well. When symptom care is deemed no longer beneficial, only comfort care and respect care are administered. Sometimes, though, only respect care is appropriate.

Added difficulty in decision making occurs when patients' conditions teeter between the categories of reversibility and irreversibility, the permanence of their unconsciousness is uncertain, or the imminence of their death is questionable (see gray ovals in Figures 2–1 and 2–2). Often a person's battle for life is measured by percentages. For example, a physician may state that an operation has a 20 percent chance of reversing an illness, or the percentages may be fifty-fifty.

Two guidelines are helpful when there is such uncertainty. First, when it is unclear which of the two categories best fits the patient's condition, and thus which types of care are most appropriate, lean toward the wider range of care. For example, if reversibility is uncertain but quite possible, lean toward curative care, which offers the widest range of care, including symptom care, comfort care, and respect care. If the imminence of a terminal, conscious patient's death is uncertain, lean toward symptom care, which includes a wider range of care than comfort care.

The second guideline is to recognize that patients (or those empowered to make medical decisions for them) are in the best position to determine what is the best course of action—with the counsel of others (see question 8). When there is uncertainty, there is a risk of harmful consequences, and it is the patient who must suffer them. Consider the situation in which rigorous chemotherapy and radiation therapy present a small chance of reversing a patient's cancer. If the therapies do not stop the cancer, they will succeed only in making the person's last few months more miserable. In such a case, the treatment rather than the disease may end up *causing* the worst suffering. So, the best course of action is not always obvious. Life-sustaining technology has provided this and future generations with the ability or misfortune of having greater choice over the timing of our deaths. We must keep in mind that medical technology is a human invention, not a divine mandate.

People, especially the community of faith, should respect the difficulty of these decisions. They should encourage patients (or their decision makers) to seek the will of God who alone sees beyond the uncertainty. The Lord is not an uncompassionate bystander, but the High Priest who can sympathize with our weaknesses and understand our struggle and desire to do what is right. "Let us therefore draw near with confidence to the throne of grace, that we may receive mercy and may find grace to help in time of need" (Heb. 4:16).

4. How do I prepare adequately for the dying process?

The most important way an individual can prepare for the dying process is to become personally acquainted with the One who entered our human state as a child in Bethlehem. To know Jesus Christ as one's Savior from sin takes down the wall that separates us from God and abolishes the fear of death and the threat of eternal judgment. However, it does not abolish our apprehension of the dying process or change the manner of our dying. Jesus suffered greatly in the Garden of Gethsemane over the manner of his dying. He was deeply grieved and troubled over the unavoidable dying process that would soon consume His human existence. He fell to the ground and pleaded for His Father to intervene on His behalf (Matt. 26:39–41; Mark 14:33–36; Luke 22:41–46).

The agony of the ensuing hours until his death was the most dreadful in all of human history for the Godhead because it was in those excruciating moments that the judgment of sin found its mark on God Himself in the person of Jesus Christ. But think also of the dying process to which Christ was subjected. His palliative care (respect care) consisted of sour

21

wine soaked into a sponge and administered from the end of a branch. Had He not died after this gesture of compassion, the soldiers would have hastened His death by breaking His legs (John 19:33). It is this tragic and necessary death (cf. John 6:38) that helps separate our fear of death from the dying process. Although the physical journey through the dying process may be difficult, the spiritual existence that follows is the reward of faith.

Another way that we can prepare for the dying process is to build and maintain healthy relationships with family members (especially those closest to us, such as spouse and children), friends, and church congregations. The dying process is not only the experience of an individual, it is the experience of a community. Love throughout the healthy years, sprinkled with genuine gestures of forgiveness as needed, will guarantee that the dying process will not find the patient lonely and without support. Remember that the dying process can intrude on any member of the family at any time and at any age. Families and friends are gifts from God to be nourished and cherished so that in times of accomplishment, mutual joy is shared. And in times of tragedy, turmoil, grief, and loss, comfort and care is shared.

Don't let injured pride keep you away from those whom you need and who need you. It is unconscionable to think that family, friends, and churches let those they love, or even loathe, die alone in a hospital, surrounded by strangers whose commitment to the patient may or may not be genuine and whose technologies appear cold and sterile. It is tragic how many elderly persons "have no one who still cares," and it is disheartening that church communities believe that sending flowers and cards that express a commitment to pray for the elderly and dying can replace the touch of a hand, the closeness of a hug, the smile in a shared look, or the sound of genuine care from a mouth that can be seen.[4] Forget the flowers and send yourself, live and in person, whenever that is feasible. Remember that God came in person, in the person of Jesus Christ, to a dying world.

Make sure that your loved ones understand and are committed to upholding your desires regarding end-of-life treatment. If you enter the dying process knowing that your family or friends understand your views regarding life-sustaining technology (the conditions under which you want them applied as well as when and if you want them removed), you will have a better sense of control during a time when control is tenuous or limited.

Prior to experiencing the dying process, each of us must gain an understanding of the reality of death as not only an enemy, which it certainly is, but also as an entry—a doorway into a new dimension of life. For the Christian, it marks the completion of a task, a life of faithfulness that has come to its end. Remember the words of Jesus on the cross after He received the sour wine to ease His thirst: "'It is finished!' And He bowed His head, and gave up His spirit" (John 19:30). Through His death, He completed His journey of paving the only highway to heaven; through His resurrection, He opened that highway to human travel. Death, though tragic and unnatural, is the path to life eternal.

Consider the statement of Paul as he reflects on the end of life.

For I am already being poured out as a drink offering, and the time of my departure has come. I have fought the good fight, I have finished the course, I have kept the faith; in the future there is laid up for me the crown of righteousness, which the Lord, the righteous Judge, will award to me on that day; *and not only to me, but also to all who have loved His appearing*" (2 Tim. 4:6–8, emphasis added).

Paul had lived his life faithfully; he is not saying that he accomplished everything he might have wanted to for the Lord. But what Paul did, he did faithfully, enduring the spiritual challenges along the way. He was prepared for the dying process. We must get past the idea that at the end of life, we will have time to make our peace with God. We might as well say that forgiveness is something to be pursued only during our dying process. Death, however, doesn't sit by waiting for us to complete important details before it takes us. We can't plan to make peace with God at the end of our lives; we maintain peace with God throughout our lives. It is difficult to view death as a passageway when our lives are lived to satisfy self rather than to serve God and others.[5]

5. *Is it selfish to want to be in control during the dying process?*

The dying process comes upon us without permission. Therefore, total control is out of the question. What we are actually looking for is some *sense* of control, or better, a vital role in end-of-life decision making. The popular term used to describe patient control is *personal autonomy,* which basically means self-rule. We may worry, in today's cost-conscious environment, that we will receive less health care than we really need. We may also worry about too much treatment and prolonged suffering. We know that physicians sometimes mistakenly perceive the death of their patients as professional failure or hesitate to discontinue burdensome treatment that provides little benefit for fear of a lawsuit. Moreover, since most of us will be cared for by people we have never met, our confidence in the medical staff may be tenuous. In other words, the reasons why people desire to control end-of-life treatment are understandable and can simply reflect an appropriate desire to receive proper care.

The problem arises when our fears cause us to desire *complete control* of end-of-life health care. Most of us are not medically sophisticated enough to understand all the benefits and risks of everything that can be done medically. Too much of a desire to be in control can interfere with what is best for us, just as too little of a desire to affect what is going on could result in some form of abuse.

Therefore, it is better to think of our living and dying in terms of *interdependence* rather than autonomy. The expertise of the medical staff who take care of you is vital to your understanding of the condition that is threatening or taking your life. The staff should not be paternalistic (treating you like an ignorant child) and you, as a patient, should not be autonomous (making decisions apart from their impact on others). Together, you, the physician, the nurses, your family, clergy, friends, and others form a team whose corporate knowledge of you and your condition is far greater than your own understanding. This team can provide great comfort during what can be an extremely unsettling time. Death need not and should not be an experience we face alone. We live in relationships that involve responsibilities for ourselves and others, and we die with similar responsibilities. In the process of dying, love still teaches us to care for others and not just for ourselves. Christ taught us this principle as he reached out to meet the needs of his grieving mother and the dying thief during his own dying process.

6. Should I consider organ donation, and if so, when?

National surveys suggest that the gap between the number of people who need organ transplants and the number of organ donors continues to widen[6] even though an increase in prospective donors has been reported between 1988 and 1996. While increases have occurred in all age groups, donations from people over age fifty have increased significantly.[7] Because the end-of-life experience can take place at any age and because younger donors are less likely to have their organs discarded, it is important that serious discussions about the willingness to donate organs take place as early as possible—as early as eighteen years of age.[8] Prior to this, parents must consider the maturity level of their children. Parents need not intrude upon children with such serious discussions because the decision to use the organs of children, in the event of death, lies with the parents.

While all do not agree,[9] it would seem wise for all adults to make decisions regarding organ donation in cooperation with family members (or, when necessary, with significant others). Such is the case whether or not a "mandatory choice" law is adopted in the United States.[10] Moreover, if it is possible to include a physician in the discussion, one is prudent to do so.[11] At present, it appears that physicians are ignoring advance directives (see question 13) regarding an individual's determination to donate one's organs and are placing ultimate responsibility for the decision on the family members at the time of a loved one's death. Too often family members are unable or unwilling to comply with the advance directive of their loved one; they may even be taken aback by the suggestion because they were unaware of the loved one's desire to donate.[12]

When you give an organ to another individual, you perform a service as great as that of any physician because you give sight to the blind, life to those who need a beating heart, or breath to those whose lungs falter. You bring relief from impending loss and, often, incessant pain. You also give a fellow human being greater opportunity to live life, hopefully, more abundantly if through an extended life he or she comes to know the giver of all life, the Lord Himself. Those of us who know the Lord can look forward to His return when our perished and decayed remains are raised from the dead and transformed into whole and imperishable bodies—the physical and mortal replaced with a spiritual and immortal body (1 Cor. 15:42–54; cf. 1 Thess. 4:13–17). Our organs are a part of the earth, a part of our natural bodies, and are, therefore, perishable. Only through donation can these organs continue to serve a useful and more lasting purpose. Our spiritual bodies, which are neither flesh and blood nor mortal, will have no need of them (1 Cor. 15:50).

7. If I am old or disabled or my quality of life is low, is my life of less value?

Age and quality of life may determine your ability to do a job, but they have nothing whatsoever to do with the immense significance you have as a member of the human race. Even speaking of life in terms of how much "value" it has improperly places life on a scale of value. It mistakenly suggests that life can be compared and traded off with other things of value. Life is not negotiable in this way. Life is life! Ultimately people's significance does not rest in mobility and function; rather, it rests in the creative hands of He who made us as His image bearers (Gen. 1:26–27; 9:6).

The significance of a human being is established by God, not by humanity. This fact lies at the heart of every ethical debate that is created by the advancement of medical technology. It is essential that we do not underestimate the truth that "men and women, in their very nature, reflect something of the dignity and worth of God himself."[13] Our view of God determines how we view and treat each other and ourselves. God's love and concern for each of us does not fail because we are weak, less intelligent, sick, and dying and, therefore, neither should ours. Among the greatest and most successful people in our land are nurses and volunteers who have chosen to care for the dying—to respect and care for those who suffer. These caregivers have not forgotten the inherent significance of a human being.

It is true, however, that as people forget about or forsake God, they also dishonor creation, of which human beings are a major part. If something (or someone) doesn't benefit society, such people suggest that it should be discarded so that something or someone else can take its place. It is the natural conclusion of evolutionary theory that the weak do not, and even should not, survive. It also appears to be the opinion of many that if the weak, dying, and elderly are out of sight, they are also out of mind. How can we say that we respect the weak and the dying when more than three-quarters of those who die do so in hospitals and federal programs, disregarded by a fast-paced American economy that has little time for those who cannot "keep up"? They attended our churches and supported our economy with their strength and talents, but when they grew weak and fragile, churches and businesses all too often focused on their younger and stronger replacements without ensuring that care would be provided to those who had gone before. Everyone in society has put the brunt of the financial responsibility on the shoulders of the government. Although the government is helping and should continue to do so, the church and the business world have a financial responsibility (debt) to support hospice care or create facilities of their own to meet the needs of America's aging elders.

King David asked God not to cast him off "in the time of old age" and not to forsake him when his strength failed—an allusion to all-to-common behavior toward the elderly and the weak (Ps. 71:9). We, the people of God, who are the image-bearers of God, are responsible to ensure that the dignity and concerns of the weak and aging do not go unnoticed and unresolved. To ignore, cheapen or dishonor those who become weak among us is a form of oppression. To claim that we are a people of God demands that we do justice and righteousness by pleading "the cause of the afflicted and needy" (Jer. 22:15–17).

> God takes His stand in His own congregation;
> He judges in the midst of the rulers.
> How long will you judge unjustly,
> And show partiality to the wicked?
> Vindicate the weak and fatherless;
> Do justice to the afflicted and destitute.
> Rescue the weak and needy;
> Deliver them out of the hand of the wicked.
>
> (Ps. 82:1–4)

In other words, your dignity is established by God and placed under the protection of society. Your age, ability, and medical status do not affect your intrinsic dignity.

DECISION-MAKING ISSUES

8. *What are the roles of the patient, the physician, and family members in treatment decision making?*

Today decision making is much different than it was in the past. Historically, the attending physician made the medical decisions based on what he or she felt was best for the patient. Today, as long as the patient is conscious, aware (i.e., competent; compare question 10), and over the age of eighteen in most states, popular opinion suggests that decisions regarding medical treatment rest with the patient. However, a more collaborative approach is probably the best model—i.e., the physician and the patient working together to provide the best possible care. It is unrealistic and burdensome for the patient to attempt to make every medical decision autonomously. Patients can make decisions regarding whether or not they want to receive life-sustaining treatments, but decisions related to the manner in which the equipment is used to achieve the patient's desire is more a matter for the physician.[14]

For example, if a conscious eighty-five-year-old cancer patient, prior to surgery, is informed that there is a one in four chance that he will die during surgery, he might refuse the operation. However, if he accepts the risk, the technical decisions regarding the particular procedure are left to the physician. Also, the patient can agree to the operation but stipulate that if he goes into cardiac arrest, no effort is to be made to resuscitate him. The physician may consider this an unwise stipulation since the heart stoppage may just be a temporary problem that can be fixed—so a physician-patient (or physician-proxy) discussion is needed prior to surgery. The point is that end-of-life decision making should neither isolate the patient nor ignore the physician. The process is a journey through which both must travel. Mutual respect is essential to the process. Open and complete disclosure of a patient's condition with an honest prognosis (the expected impact the illness will have on the patient's life) plus the absence of coercion on the part of the physician will foster in the competent patient a trust that makes decision making a mutual endeavor.

In addition to the physician's involvement, the patient also needs the support of family members and close friends to make wise decisions. As long as they, too, are careful to avoid even subtle coercion, they can help the patient identify and weigh the many non-medical considerations that may be involved in a treatment decision. Their understanding and involvement is even more important after the patient loses the mental ability to make decisions. The patient can avoid guesswork, the intervention of the court, and conflict between the physician and family members by stating his or her treatment desires in an advance directive, such as a living will or a durable power of attorney for health care (DPAHC; see question 13). It is a good idea to make not only family members but also your closest friends aware of your end-of-life health-care preferences. In the event that no family can be reached, a friend may come forward to express your spoken concerns if written directives are unobtainable, misplaced, or ignored.

9. Who needs to know that I am dying or may be dying?

Although the knowledge of one's own death is sobering and often frightening, it is important to be aware of the extent of one's deterioration. Interdependent decision making is impossible when the major player in the process, the patient, is not involved. Advance directives (see question 13) are valid only when the patient is mentally incompetent, and they should not take the place of consulting with a patient who is still competent. Competent patients must be given the truth so that they can be knowledgeably involved in medical treatment decisions as well as choices such as whether or not to enter a hospital, where and with whom to spend their last days, and how to put their affairs in order.[15] Unless patients directly request that they not know the extent of their conditions, which is unlikely, physicians are morally responsible to tell patients the truth.

The family and friends of a dying patient also need to be informed, though not necessarily by the physician. If the patient is unconscious or otherwise mentally incompetent, the physician will need to inform the person whom the patient has designated in an advance directive (see question 13) or, if no such directive exists, the appropriate surrogate decision maker. The patient's medical condition, however, is confidential, so the physician should not reveal it to anyone other than the patient (or their surrogate decision maker) without the patient's consent. Nevertheless, patients should allow physicians to communicate with selected individuals, unless the patients prefer to do that themselves. Dying patients should not keep their imminent death from family for the same reasons that they would not want to be left out. Family and friends need time to prepare for the death, especially those who are a part of the decision-making team. End-of-life decisions are best made corporately among patient, physician, and family (see question 8). Death is more than a personal experience; it impacts many people. Therefore, all who will be significantly affected should be told. Though exceptions and reasons for delaying the notification may exist, they are few and specific to each family's situation. Exceptions, however, are not the rule and should be exercised with great caution. There is no need to cause distrust or additional grief without extraordinary justification.

The idea that the physician is protecting dying patients, or patients are protecting family members, from unwelcome news is inconsiderate of the need to begin closure of relationships and to set affairs in order. It also appears inconsistent with the Patient Self-Determination Act that the Congress of the United States passed in 1990. We live with loved ones and we should die with loved ones. Although we often fail to care for one another as consistently as we should in life, we should make every effort to care for one another as dying intrudes to temporarily separate us. May the manner in which we die be a reflection of the love that Christ desires to instill in each of us—a love that does not seek its own or act unbecomingly but rejoices in the truth (1 Cor. 13:5–6).

10. What are informed consent and mental competence?

Informed consent is the *voluntary decision* made by a mentally competent and informed adult whether to accept or reject proposed medical care. Mental competence is the legally established capacity to make and communicate decisions. For legal purposes, determinations of mental competence are the responsibility of mental-health professionals. The mental capacity required to be mentally competent has three aspects. It includes the patient's ability (1) to take in information, (2) to assess that information in relation to his or her own beliefs and values, and (3) to communicate the resulting decisions to another person.

The nature of the information the patient must receive and the detailed disclosure of risks and possible outcomes of a particular course of care or treatment has been measured against one of two models: the physician-oriented approach, or the consumer-based approach. Traditionally, the amount and specificity of information given have been judged under a "reasonable physician" model. That is, what would a reasonable physician disclose in the same or similar circumstances? A subspecialty physician in a teaching hospital may give details that would not be expected of a family practitioner in a community hospital. This somewhat patriarchal model is being replaced by a patient-oriented model: What would a reasonable consumer need to know in order to make an intelligent decision? Increasingly, sophisticated patients are demanding details about the proposed procedure, about other courses of treatment, and about the integration of alternative medicine.

More than the provision of information to a mentally competent patient is necessary, though, for an "informed consent" to be truly ethical. The patient needs not only to *receive* sufficient information (perhaps signing a form that contains all the details), but also to *understand* it. To determine if this condition has been met, any caregiver or friend can simply ask the patient what he or she has consented to and why. If the patient cannot provide a reasonable explanation, he or she may well not have given *informed* consent.

Finally, to be ethical the informed consent must be free from coercion on the part of the physician, family, and others. Even subtle coercive influences, such as economics, should be eliminated to the degree possible. In this regard, the very name, *informed consent,* is unfortunate. It implies that the patient will always consent to what the physician proposes. This need not be the case as, for example, when the patient weighs the conflicting medical and nonmedical considerations differently than does the physician.[16]

Minors are legally incompetent to make their own decisions regarding medical care (except for matters deemed to be protected by their right to privacy, such as contraception and abortion). Informed consent must therefore be given by the parent or legal guardian. However, if a minor is freed from parental control (usually by marriage) or is mature (as determined by a judge), he or she may give or withhold consent to medical treatment. For example, when minors object to blood transfusions on religious grounds, their nonconsent may be sufficient.

11. Do I have a legal right to determine my medical treatment?

Unless you are a minor or incompetent (see questions 10 and 15), you have a legal right to determine your own medical treatment. It is a clearly recognized legal principle that a competent adult has a virtually unlimited right to refuse even life-sustaining medical treatment.[17] This right is based on common-law principles of informed consent and protection against battery. A patient has a right to be fully informed of the procedure and risks before consenting to any medical treatment (see question 10). If consent is not given, the doctor or medical professional could be liable for battery.

Even patients who are incompetent have the right to *refuse* medical treatment if there is clear evidence that they would not want to continue to live under such circumstances. If there is no such evidence, treatment might still be withdrawn legally if the patient is in a persistent vegetative state, or in other cases where the patient is not competent.[18] The propriety of such withdrawal depends on the particular facts of the case.

This comprehensive right to refuse includes all forms of medical treatment, even though death is the certain outcome of withdrawal. Some parties will seek withdrawal of nutrition and hydration as a form of unconsented or unwanted medical treatment. More often, the issues revolve around medical interventions such as a respirator, resuscitation, and feeding tubes.

Refusing medical treatment is *not* the same thing as committing suicide, and the caregiver who complies with the patient's wishes is *not* assisting a suicide. Legally, there is a clear distinction "between directly *causing* death by an affirmative act ending life and *allowing* death to occur by withholding or withdrawing life-sustaining medical treatment."[19]

However, the right to determine one's medical treatment is not unlimited. A person cannot demand medically unnecessary treatment, such as amputation of a limb or hospitalization for wart removal. A physician is not merely a technician who can be ordered to carry out a person's wishes. Physicians are obligated to practice medicine ethically, according to the standards of their specialties and the medical community within which they practice.

12. What treatment and financial plans should I make while I am still healthy?

We commonly put off to the end what comes at the end. The problem is that end-of-life issues may not wait until our other priorities are complete. In fact, end-of-life concerns are actually immediate concerns, in that you may fall ill or may be seriously injured tomorrow. Knowing that one day your spouse, your children, or your friends will care for you as you die, you must ensure, as best you can, that they know your treatment preferences and the manner in which your dying can be financially managed. Although your ability to provide adequate financial stability is dependent on income, employment benefits, supplemental insurance, and accumulated or inherited assets, there is no excuse for your family's not knowing your end-of-life treatment preferences. Along with an advance directive (see question 13), prepare a will with a lawyer (or with a guidebook or legal-software programs) that spells out who will inherit your assets. To maximize the resources available for loved ones, it is also often important before death to set up legal trusts for your assets and to redistribute ownership of assets between spouses and among adults and their children. Seek legal advice on these issues.

Don't confuse a will with an advance directive—you need both. Once you have acquired an advance directive, mail copies of it to all "need to know" individuals. These include not only your physician and the person whom you want to make medical decisions for you should you become mentally incompetent but also other close family members. Don't forget to include those whom you believe might make the surrogate decision maker's job difficult if they are upset by any of the provisions of your advance directive. If you update the directive, be sure to redistribute the updated document to all who have the previous version. Be sure the signed and witnessed original is in a safe place and that the location is known at least to your spouse or the executor of your estate (the executor will be identified in your will).

Another important preparation is to make an appointment with a funeral home to prearrange your burial. This appointment and the advance purchase of a lot or crematorium space at a cemetery can greatly reduce the overall end-of-life expense. Leaving this responsibility to your loved ones at the time of your death adds undue stress to an already stressful experience. Loved ones who are caring for a terminally ill family member who has not made these funeral arrangements, though it may seem awkward, should make burial arrangements before the person dies. Learn, and honor, the wishes of the dying loved one if possible. It is easier to avoid being drawn into purchasing a burial that is beyond your means if you make plans in advance of the emotional crisis that typically accompanies a loved one's death.

It is disappointing that one's entire life's savings can end up in the pockets of a health maintenance organization, health care professionals, the government, and others. To hopefully avoid this, financial planning is essential. Once you are unable to work, Social Security payments from the government can provide some income, but Social Security is not enough to handle all the needs that a terminal illness can create. It generally amounts to between $1,000 and $1,500 and isn't immediately available—you may have to wait months before receiving your first payment. Social Security will also not be paid unless you are unable to do "substantial work," which is work that pays you more than $500 a month.

If you carry disability insurance with your employer or have purchased it yourself, check to see when you can begin receiving its benefits. Remember that disability payments from coverage paid by an employer is taxable while payments from coverage purchased individually is not. A physician must confirm that you are unable to remain employed at your present job. Check with your employer or insurance agent to learn about other benefits that you may have with disability insurance.

Group life-insurance policies with employers may be convertible, within thirty-one days from the time you give notice, to an individual policy on which you must pay the premium. It is expensive, but this *may* be the only life insurance option remaining for you. If you have less than six months to live, the expense for this life insurance is well worth the financial benefit that the policy will provide those you leave behind. If you have health insurance through an employer, you can continue this coverage when you stop working, but you must pay the full nongroup rate in compliance with a United States federal program called the Consolidated Omnibus Budget Reconciliation Act, better known as COBRA. (As of this writing, this program ensures availability of coverage for eighteen months with the possibility of an extension to twenty-nine months if you are disabled.) If you have your own life or health insurance, see your agent if you are not sure what benefits are included in your policy. For example, you may have purchased a waiver-of-premium rider that allows you to continue coverage under certain conditions without having to continue paying the premium.[20]

Don't forget hospice care. If you qualify (see question 29), hospice can help relieve a tremendous amount of the financial, physical, emotional, and spiritual burden. Medicare does not require that you forfeit your assets as a prerequisite to entering the hospice program. Also, some not-for-profit hospices are able to provide care for terminally ill patients who have less than six months to live and are without insurance (thanks to fund-raising programs, scholarships, and donations).

The cost of insurance and medical care is regrettably enormous. It is disheartening that the business of responding to human suffering seems more based on profit margins than on compassion. Nonetheless, we must do what we can to ease the burden on others that is caused by our own deaths or the deaths of those we love. Maintaining life insurance when we have dependents or starting annuities or mutual funds in our youth to care for those left behind at our death are wise parts of our financial planning. Wills protect our assets. Advance directives direct our end-of-life care. Health and disability insurance often come through employment, but if not, they should be acquired at the level to which you are financially able to afford them. Although we cannot know or direct the future, our love for family forces us to prepare for it. Speaking to those who have the means, Paul writes, "But if anyone does not provide for his own, and especially for those of his household, he has denied the faith" (1 Tim. 5:8). To live without concern for the effect our lives and deaths have on friends and family is inconsistent with faith in God. The dying process is as much a part of life as finding a place to live—both require planning if they are to turn out well.

13. What are advance directives?

An advance directive is a legally authorized document that enables a person to make certain decisions about his or her future health care. The laws regarding advance directives vary from state to state. The implementation of advance directives may also be governed by hospital procedures, ethics committees, and the specific circumstances of the case.

There are several types of advance directives, including both a living will and a durable power of attorney for health care. These can include specific details or may be quite general. They also can be written, oral (when used as evidence of a patient's wishes where no other evidence exists), or videotaped.

Some states prescribe a specific form. Other documents, which may not follow a specific form, might also be evidence of the patient's wishes. To that extent, these documents could be viewed as advance directives. Some states specifically limit the effect of advance directives. Other states more broadly permit the application of all advance directives.

One common written directive is a *living will*. A living will is your written statement that delineates what medical treatment you want or do not want should you become incapacitated and unable to speak for yourself. State laws vary as to the limitations on treatment that are allowed, so ensure that your desires comply with the laws in the state in which you reside. As of this writing, living wills are legal in all states except Massachusetts, Michigan, and New York. They generally are operative only when there has been a determination of terminal illness or imminent death or the diagnosis of a persistent vegetative state (PVS). A durable power of attorney for health care (DPAHC) is a document that names a particular person or series of people to make medical decisions on your behalf if you become mentally incompetent (see question 10). A person so designated is sometimes called your proxy, surrogate, health-care agent, or attorney-in-fact. DPAHCs are authorized by the Durable Power of Attorney for Health Care Act or a natural death/living will statute. The durable power of attorney differs from a living will in that it does not spell out medical treatment. A DPAHC is often used to implement a living will by naming a particular person or alternates to convey the patient's desires and directing them to carry out the instructions of the living will. A DPAHC is legal in all states except Alaska, which authorizes only the living will.

None of these advance directives is self-executing. Some person must produce the document, and it must be accepted as a genuine, uncoerced expression of the patient's wishes.[21] However, even when a detailed advance directive is available, it does not, in and of itself, dictate medical decisions. The physician may consult with family members, other physicians, the hospital ethics committee, nursing staff, clergy, and others, particularly if the certain outcome is the death of the patient.

14. Are advance directives a good idea?

Many people, including Christians, have understandably resisted the living will as ethically problematic. Some are concerned that living wills were first developed by organizations as a strategic step toward fulfilling a broad euthanasia agenda. This historical fact alone, though, should not cause one to reject living wills out of hand but rather to examine them much more carefully on their own merits. Some people have done precisely that—scrutinized them critically—and found them to be dangerous. Because people can never anticipate all possible future scenarios, living wills can easily give permission to withhold or withdraw treatment under unique circumstances in which a person would actually want such treatment.

For this reason, a second form of advance directive has gained favor: a durable power of attorney for health care. It is not a perfect vehicle, but it provides the best means available to ascertain the wishes and values of a patient without mental capacity. Such a person's wishes and values should still be respected because he or she remains a living human being.

If people want to put some of their wishes and values in a living will (or a living will section of a durable power of attorney for health care document), that information may prove helpful to their surrogate decision makers. Such information can include not only concerns about avoiding overtreatment—the reason for which living wills arose—but also, increasingly, concerns about avoiding undertreatment. Employed in this latter way, living-will provisions work directly to counter the drift toward euthanasia that those concerned about advance directives fear. Nevertheless, people should explicitly state that any living-will-type information in their advance directive(s) is advisory only and that the judgments of their surrogates are final. People must also communicate the existence of their advance directives to their family members and primary caregivers—an often-neglected final step that commonly renders advance directives ineffective.

If you do not establish an advance directive prior to your illness, the Patient Self-Determination Act has made it mandatory for hospitals in the United States to advise you of your right to refuse medical treatment should your condition become hopeless or irreversible.

Please keep in mind, however, that hospitals cannot receive end-of-life treatment directions from a patient who is unable to communicate. Remember: "Most people know someone whose dying seemed to go awry, *whether through injudicious overtreatment or inadequate supportive care services* (emphasis added). The limited data available support the pervasiveness of these anecdotes."[22] Therefore, it is critical that every person who expects to experience the dying process (that's all of us) develop an advance directive— preferably one done on a form specified in state law; however, if you prefer not to obtain a legal document, a signed (preferably witnessed) personal memo is better than nothing at all.

Nevertheless, we should be realistic about how consistently physicians will honor advance directives. Information gathered in 1992 suggested that 75 percent of the treatment that patients received was consistent with their advance directives. This relatively high rate of consistency was most likely due to a similarity of values between patient and physician. "It appeared that the patient's preferences were respected as long as the physicians thought that the patient's choices resulted in the best decisions."[23] In other words, if the physician did not agree with the patient's determination, it was less likely that the directive would be followed. In 1997, *The New England Journal of Medicine* reported that physicians and nurses, when "[f]orced to choose between what they were trained to do and what they were never trained to do, may continue aggressive therapy well beyond the point at which patients or families (or the health care professionals themselves) would prefer to stop."[24]

Probably the best you can do is to prepare an advance directive and ensure that its contents are known to your doctor, your family, and your friends. If the physician does not agree or refuses to comply with the stipulations you place in the directive, make a genuine effort to understand his or her concerns. If agreement cannot be reached, get another primary physician. Physicians need to know that carrying out the patient's wishes, if clearly expressed in the advance directive, does not implicate the medical staff in assisting suicide. State legislators and court decisions have been careful to clearly distinguish between a person's exercising the right to refuse medical treatment and assisting or committing suicide. If anything, physicians should be particularly concerned about overtreating patients against their wishes, especially in the United States. Recently the states of Michigan (*Osgood v. Genesys Regional Medical Center*, March, 1997) and Ohio (*Anderson v. St. Francis-St. George Hospital*, October, 1996) charged physicians with battery when they performed medical procedures that were in violation of an advocate's direction and a do-not-resuscitate order respectively.[25] Advance directives are designed to protect the patient from unwanted technological intrusion. It is disappointing to see legal judgments, whose rewards will create greater costs to medical care, become the impetus for bringing about adherence to a patient's end-of-life treatment desires. Since most of the difficulties surrounding advance directives involve no ill will on the part of physicians, patients, or others, good communication in advance is essential to having one's end-of-life treatment decisions honored.[26]

15. Who makes treatment decisions for an incompetent patient with no advance directive?

If you choose to have neither form of advance directive, you should tell close family members and friends what end-of-life procedures you would prefer were you to become incapacitated in a terminal state. Without direction, the medical community is forced to do what it thinks is best. Don't put your family in the unnecessary and emotionally draining legal position of having to fight over the manner of your treatment during the dying process. When the patient has left no advance directive, the decision maker may be determined by state law. Usually, the physician consults with the spouse. If there is no surviving spouse, then the next closest relatives, such as children or parents, are typically consulted. The hospital medical-ethics committee may also review treatment decisions if withdrawal of life-sustaining treatment is contemplated.

There are two risks that accompany not having an advance directive. First, those without advance directives cannot be as confident about the treatment they will receive. Second, as society continues to develop a greater openness to suicide and euthanasia (see *Suicide and Euthanasia* book in this series), health care will no longer be concerned solely with restoring and sustaining life but also with ending it. In the Netherlands, which has allowed euthanasia for a number of years,[27] the lives of a significant number of incompetent patients have been ended without their consent. Therefore, leaving the type of medical intervention and care in the hands of people whose values differ from your own is risky. Your life may be prematurely ended.

Building on a legitimate fear of an unnecessarily demeaning dying process, proponents of physician-assisted suicide (PAS) have found a way to promote "mercy killings."[28] Although some PAS proponents are motivated by compassion, the inherent dignity of each human life and the psychological mistrust that this "solution" will generate between patients and the medical community requires us to pursue an alternative that promotes care, not killing. Much of the medical community has felt the pressure of the PAS movement and is presently responding by creating educational programs and seminars for physicians in need of end-of-life or palliative care training.[29] One of the issues in their training involves the purpose and use of advance directives.

16. When is hospitalization appropriate?

Human life is a loan from God that is to be used for the glory of God in the context of community. The self alone is incomplete—we are people who need relationships to discover the significance and purpose of our lives. To be created in the image of God involves both divine purpose to which we must devote ourselves and moral obligation that helps guide how we pursue that purpose. To achieve God's purpose(s) for our lives (which will not always be completely clear to us), we must live a life span known only to God, and we must live that life depending on God in a just, righteous, and faithful manner (see 1 Cor. 4:2; 6:18–20).

Each of us does many things to maintain our lives. We work to have funds to buy food, we go to a store for food, we exercise so we can work longer and eventually retire. Throughout this maintenance program, we go to the clinic or hospital for checkups and, sometimes, for fairly serious overhauls. We do this to live, or better, to bring glory to God—to help us accomplish whatever purpose(s) He desires of us. Therefore, generally speaking, we should avail ourselves of the medical benefits that help keep our frail bodies functioning. While that may mean seeking hospital care, it may also mean moving to a long-term care facility (see question 17) where medical care and other support services are immediately available.

Eventually, not even a wise maintenance program will keep the body from moving into the final phase of the dying process when death is imminent (see question 2). At this point, end-of-life issues take precedence. Both we and our physicians must come to accept the fact that we have completed everything God wants to accomplish with us (or at least all that we will allow Him to accomplish) except for what He wants to do in and through us during our journey at the end of the dying process. Don't forget that you have opportunity to fellowship with Him and to positively influence others until the moment of your death.

In the last months and days of your life, you can arrange for home health care. Such care includes the freedom to withhold and withdraw life-prolonging technology (see question 3). Stay in touch with your physician so that you receive the proper palliative care (comfort care; see question 28) to ease any pain that may develop. If conditions permit and you prefer to die at home, this environment will provide a surrounding that is more familiar and friendly. Peace is more easily experienced among family and friends than it is with strangers.

When Ruth gave birth to Obed, the women in the

community prayed that he would be to Naomi, his grandmother, a "restorer of life and a sustainer of [her] old age" (Ruth 4:15). In our very mobile societies, we have lost the connectedness of family from one generation to another and the care that such proximity brings. This separation has forced us to search for others outside of the family to care for our aging and dying family members. If hospital costs require us to come together as families and look after one another more closely, they have done us a favor. Holding the hands of our loved ones while they die in the comfort of their own home will not scar us or our children emotionally—it might actually heal us.

Contact your insurance company to ensure that they cover home-care costs. If they don't, you might investigate the possibility of getting a new insurance policy. A good case for end-of-life home care can certainly be made. In one study, half the seriously ill persons who died spent all of their final week on a respirator in an intensive-care unit. Curtailing such treatment, when morally justifiable, might well finance many home visits and other supportive care.[30] The choice to die at home is reasonable. Make sure your family or others involved in your care know your desire to die at home in the event your last moments leave you incoherent.

Keep in mind that more and more hospitals are offering palliative-care programs for the dying. If you need or prefer to go to a hospital for end-of-life care, know that many facilities are creating environments that are more homelike. More health-care professionals understand that modern medicine must provide a quiet environment with soft lighting and music that allows physical contact with the patient so that the patient, family, and friends may experience the "separation process" of dying more privately and in a less sterile setting than that of a hospital ward or intensive-care unit.[31] Have a meeting with the social-services department of your hospital to learn what it offers regarding end-of-life care.

17. What is long-term care?

Whether the condition of patients is reversible or irreversible, both convalescence (gradual healing that occurs with curative care) or the provision of symptom care during the dying process often require long-term care. Such care cannot be provided in a hospital because of the high cost. Accordingly, long-term care is defined as the extended provision of health care and other forms of care to patients whose conditions require some form of care beyond hospitalization. Four of the major categories of long-term care are nursing home care, hospice care, home health care, and home care.[32]

Nursing home care operates at three levels, depending on the needs of patients. Patients who need twenty-four-hour attention receive skilled nursing care from a registered nurse under the supervision of a physician who is available in the event of an emergency. Patients whose care does not require round-the-clock monitoring receive intermediate nursing care. Finally, those who require only room and board and occasional personal care receive custodial care. This third group of patients generally do not require health-care services. Be sure to visit your local nursing home to see how it manages each of these levels of care and to determine the exact cost for each level.

Hospice care offers physicians, skilled nursing,

and a variety of volunteer assistance to meet the needs of terminally ill patients, typically those whose death will likely occur within six months. This care takes place in specialized hospice facilities or at home. Hospice care considers the needs of the whole person: physical, mental, emotional, and spiritual. Federally certified hospices receive government funding. For further details, see question 29.

Home health care covers a wide variety of services offered at home, sometimes under a physician's supervision. Nurses, physical therapists, and personal-care assistants work together to provide medical services and assistance with grooming and dressing— all in the comfort of the patient's home. Costs are based on an hourly rate for personal-care assistants and per visit (one to two hours) for a registered nurse or a therapist. Check with Medicare to determine which medical services received at home qualify for financial aid.

Home care offers only nonmedical services in a home setting. These services include assistance in minor household maintenance as well as cleaning and yard work. The cost for these services is minimal (hourly rates) and includes materials. Local programs such as Meals on Wheels will provide food service once or twice a day directly to the home of patients. These meals can be delivered five days a week and are generally under $5 per meal. Other home-care programs include the services of volunteers who will visit patients at home, help them with errands around town, and assist them in writing letters. Local religious or volunteer groups often offer these services. Your community may have a telephone reassurance program run by volunteers who make or receive daily calls from elderly patients living alone. Finally, to protect your loved one, you may want to look into acquiring an emergency response system that is operated by telephone or by an electronic device.

Check with your physician about long-term care that may be available in your community. Check also with your pastor to learn if any churches in your community provide long-term care services. You can locate information for many of these services in the Yellow Pages or on the Community Services page in the front of your phone book. Patients don't have to be alone. There are numerous local civic, religious, and government programs working to make life at its end humane, comfortable, and even enjoyable.

TERMINATION OF LIFE-SUPPORT

18. What is a "do not resuscitate" (DNR) order, and when is it appropriate?

A DNR order is a written statement that no effort should be made to revive the heart or lungs if the patient's heartbeat or breathing stops—in other words, no cardiopulmonary resuscitation (CPR). This order signals the patient's complete acceptance of, or acquiescence to, death and may be appropriate for a terminally ill patient whose death is imminent (see question 3). The physician is responsible to discuss with patients their goals and the treatment options that are consistent with those goals. Such goals may include a peaceful death, as opposed to employing every available technology to the bitter end. Without a

DNR order, issued by the attending physician, medical personnel are responsible to use all methods at their disposal to sustain the life of the patient, even if the patient is clearly dying soon anyway.

It is unsettling for a patient to receive information regarding DNR orders. Often patients are uneasy with the discussion because it implies, whether intended or not, that they are in a potentially perilous medical condition that may result in abandonment, disability, and death. A study released in 1996 showed that the discussion between the physician and the patient about DNR procedures lacked sufficient information to allow patients to make an informed decision. No physician clearly described the likelihood of survival with cardiopulmonary resuscitation and most conveyed risk and benefit through only vague expressions of probability. In fact, only 13 percent discussed the potential outcomes of cardiopulmonary resuscitation. They rarely asked about the patient's personal values to help place the DNR discussion into a context more easily understood by the patient. The study also showed that physicians demonstrated few empathetic comments, and often pursued their own agendas of encouraging DNR decisions instead of responding to patient concerns.[33]

These two concerns—patients' anxiety and physicians' limited disclosures—suggest that someone from the immediate family or a patient-chosen proxy be present, if possible, when the physician and patient discuss end-of-life treatment plans. If you as a close family member or proxy miss this meeting or discover that one has not taken place, request to have a discussion with the physician as soon as possible. Remember that this discussion is legally mandatory only when a patient is admitted to the hospital "for a serious illness in which an arrest would not be unlikely and when the patient has a chronic illness and his or her condition might deteriorate."[34] Don't assume that the patient has included a DNR preference in an advance directive; treatment plans that are established in accordance with an advance directive may or may not include a DNR order.[35]

The acceptance of a DNR order by the patient *is not* an order to the medical staff to abandon the patient's care. Supportive comfort care and respect care (see question 2) from the medical staff and the immediate family will continue in the form of medications and personal presence. This may take place in the hospital or at home if the patient prefers to die in the company of his or her closest companions (see question 16). A DNR order limits, at the request of the patient, the use of a potentially life-sustaining technique that will have no lasting benefit and will only prolong unavoidable dying. Generally, when physicians consider a DNR to be appropriate, they believe that CPR is unlikely to be successful in any case. However, before deciding to request a DNR order, seek information from the physician regarding all possible benefits and harms likely to occur in you or your loved one's specific situation if CPR is attempted.

19. Should I be cautious about initiating life support for fear that removal may be difficult?

Two things must be said here: You have reason to be cautious, but you should not be overly cautious. First, you have reason to be cautious because some physicians (and family members) are reluctant to stop life-prolonging measures (a respirator, kidney dialysis, and so forth) until a patient is dead. In their minds, withholding [or withdrawing] life support is necessarily problematic because they define it as "the considered decision to not institute [or continue] a medically appropriate and possibly beneficial therapy."[36] There are situations, however, in which the use of life support is not necessarily the "medically appropriate" choice to make (see question 3). The definition itself is biased toward the overuse of life-sustaining technology. Even though physicians are becoming more sensitive to the wishes of their patients, surveys still suggest that "dying patients in hospitals in the United States frequently receive unwanted interventions."[37] So, you do have reason to be cautious.

Second, however, you should not be overly cautious. Rather than not initiating life support at all, a better approach would be to begin life-sustaining intervention for *a trial period*. Once the intervention has been tried, the physicians and patients will be able to determine accurately whether or not the treatment is appropriate and beneficial. If the patient agrees to this "time trial" and everyone involved understands the thinking behind it, a more informed consent to continuing or withdrawing the intervention is possible. If the intervention does not accomplish what is desired, the physician should honor a patient's decision to withdraw. Admittedly, withdrawing treatment already begun is more difficult psychologically for physicians than initially withholding it, but it is not more problematic ethically. Even when treatment is initiated without a time trial, physicians generally have a better basis for decision making because patients have already been experiencing the treatment in question for a while. But withdrawal is easier if a prearranged time trial has expired and a decision can be made not to reauthorize more treatment—much the same way that a medicine is not continued after the initial prescription if it does not prove effective. So, be cautious but not overly cautious.

20. What factors should a patient, a family, or other decision makers consider before deciding to terminate life support?

Understanding the dying process requires that we ask at least three questions. First, what is the diagnosis? We need to know what disease or condition has invaded. Second, what medical interventions are possible? We need to learn whether the condition is reversible or irreversible and what forms of curative or symptom care (see question 3) may be appropriate. Third, what is the prognosis of the condition with and without treatment? We need to determine how long and how well we can expect to live with each of the possible medical interventions, or with none at all. Determining if you or your loved one is dying is important because the sanctity of life does not require those who are irreversibly soon dying to prolong that dying with all available means. It does demand, however, that dying patients be allowed to die in the most humane and painless manner possible.

If a treatment will reverse the condition and restore health, by all means pursue treatment. If a treatment will not reverse the condition but will keep death at bay for a significant length of time and allow you to continue to interact with the world, pursue the treatment.[38] However, if the treatment will not reverse the condition, and death is at hand, you may accept the dying process along with the comfort care and respect care that are appropriate for your condition (see question 3).[39] Patient goals should take precedence over technological availability—just because a service can be done doesn't mean that it must be done. *Technology was made for people and not people for technology.* This understanding of technology paraphrases the statement made by Jesus: "Sabbath was made for man, and not man for the Sabbath" (Mark 2:27).

Although care should be provided by the family to their elderly loved ones, there is no reason to lengthen this difficult period of intimate involvement inappropriately, especially when the death of the loved one is imminent. Fear of death or feelings of guilt among family members do not justify prolonging the dying process, whether the patient is a believer or not. Please remember that we, as caregivers of the weak, plant and water through our faithful service, but it is God and God alone who causes the spiritual growth of the person for whom we provide care (1 Cor. 3:6-9). We are called to love those who know the Lord and those who don't. We are not responsible for bringing dying patients to their knees by prolonging death until they repent. We are His image—reflections of His character—not His Holy Spirit.

It is also not necessary to approach the decision with the fear that you may make a terrible mistake. Impending death, if it does nothing else, should bring us to our knees in prayer. "But if any of you lacks wisdom, let him ask of God, who gives to all men generously and without reproach [without a desire to find fault], and it will be given to him. But . . . ask in faith without any doubting" (James 1:5–6a). You, your loved ones, your pastor, and the medical staff know your condition better than anyone else, except God. He is in control and wants you to involve Him in the dying process. Don't forget that the heavenly Father knows what it is like to experience the death of a Son. He empathizes with your pain and understands the sense of loss. Be confident that He will guide you and provide you with the wisdom necessary to handle the challenge at hand. "Every situation is different, every person is unique. So when it comes to the 'pull the plug' question, don't waste your time looking for a tidy list of rules—one-two-three."[40] Listen to your physician, listen to God, listen to your pastor, listen to God, listen to your friends, listen to God, then trust your heart ("in abundance of counselors there is victory"—Proverbs 11:14).

Throughout this process keep an attentive eye on the motives of your heart! It is difficult to trust a heart that does not consider the welfare of others as it seeks its own. You must ask yourself how your death, or that of your loved one, will impact everyone closely involved with the situation. Sincerity of faith and a decision made corporately with those close to the crisis will greatly diminish the possibility of a self-centered decision.

21. If I remove life support, am I responsible for the death?

There is no meaningful medical, legal, or ethical difference between withholding life-sustaining technology and withdrawing it, and none of the advance-directive laws delineate between the two. People have a constitutional right to request the withdrawal or withholding of medical treatment, even if doing so will result in death.[41] As a legal matter, the courts are presently distinguishing between physician-assisted suicide, which is illegal virtually everywhere, and withdrawing or withholding life support, which is legal.

Morally, people are not responsible for the death of another if they don't *cause* it or *intend* it. When life support is removed, the illness or injury—not the withdrawal—is the medical cause of death. Nevertheless, withdrawal can be done with the primary intent of bringing on death sooner—i.e., the same problematic intent involved in assisted suicide and euthanasia (see question 15). Or, withdrawal can be done with the praiseworthy intent of allowing a loved one to die without the added burden of a medically prolonged dying process (i.e., when the condition is irreversible and death is imminent; see question 3).

Some people feel guilty after making a decision to withdraw life support because something between the patient and the decision maker was left unresolved or because they had not discussed the patient's treatment desires prior to an injury that left the patient suddenly unconscious. The quality of our relationships and our ability to communicate have much to do with the difficulty that we have in making and executing end-of-life decisions. How we love one another throughout our lives will determine the way in which we emotionally handle the decisions during the dying and death experience. However, the fact of the matter remains: A decision to terminate end-of-life technology need not be a decision to kill, but rather may be a decision to accept the inappropriateness of continued medical intervention.

Such removal of life support is *not* playing God.

Remember, medical intervention is a human invention, not a divine mandate. Using medical intervention should always benefit the patient; when it is of no use, it should be removed. God has given each of us a certain amount of time on this earth. Because we cannot know the exact time of death, we are responsible to make decisions that honor life and please God. Honoring life and pleasing God includes knowing when efforts to continue life are futile. The Scripture often reminds us of the brevity or fragility of life and the frustration that accompanies it (Ps. 90:10). James tells us that each of our lives is as a "vapor that appears for a little time and then vanishes away" (James 4:14), and Isaiah compares our flesh to grass—though it has a moment of beauty, eventually it withers and fades away (Isa. 40:6–10). As death draws near, we are under no obligation to fight unceasingly as if we could conquer it. We will never overcome death until Christ returns. So until that time, we must use the gift of medical intervention as a tool that sustains life, improves health, and provides comfort.

22. Is it ever ethical to withhold fluids and nutrition?

As long as patients are able to eat or drink (i.e., swallow and digest), you should give food and drink to them. They are "the hungry" and "the thirsty" for whom Scripture calls us to provide (Matt. 25:37–46). The dying process, however, is characterized by a shutdown of various bodily systems, including the digestive system, and we must be careful that we are not merely making dying more difficult. When the digestive system fails, the only option available is "artificial nutrition and hydration" (special liquid food and water delivered directly into the digestive canal or elsewhere in the body mechanically—e.g., through an inserted tube). As with any mechanical intervention to replace a part of the body that fails (e.g., a respirator to deliver air when the lungs cannot function on their own), you should follow the criteria for ethical intervention (see question 3). If the potentially fatal condition of patients is reversible, you should provide artificial nutrition and hydration to sustain them while curative treatment is working. If their condition is irreversible, they are conscious or potentially conscious, and their death is not imminent, they should receive artificial nutrition and hydration as part of symptom care.

If they are imminently dying with or without interventions, then artificial nutrition and hydration should be provided only when they provide comfort care to those who can experience comfort or respect care to those who cannot. During a dying patient's last days, the digestive system normally shuts down— thereby gradually weakening and diminishing alertness. Care must be taken not to start or continue artificial nutrition and hydration when they cannot alter the imminence of death but can only add to the patient's experience of pain or simply add the discomfort of a tube inserted into the body.

Another risk of continued hydration is possible fluid overload, which can cause the patient great distress. A growing consensus among health-care professionals suggests that dying patients "experience little if any discomfort upon the withdrawal of tube feedings, parenteral nutrition [taken into the body in a manner other than the digestive canal], or intravenous hydration."[42] Moreover, when artificial hydration is withheld or withdrawn, satisfactory comfort can often be provided through the mouth. As deterioration in the dying process continues, family members or medical staff can apply ice chips to moisten the patient's lips. While imminently dying, permanently unconscious patients are not conscious of pain, by definition, and so do not need comfort care, though they are still due respect care, which can include preventing the visible deterioration of their mouth and lips by keeping them moist.

In the perplexing case of permanently unconscious patients who are not imminently dying (where the meaning of *permanently* can be satisfactorily established), the same considerations and guidelines apply as explained in question 3. While artificial nutrition and hydration will be continued by many, others should be granted the liberty not to continue it in accordance with these guidelines. The uncomfortableness of some at this point is understandable because they consider artificial nutrition and hydration to be food and water with symbolic value. For them, it represents the minimum nurturing support that every member of the human community is due until the moment of death.

In the end, however, justifying the use of artificial nutrition and hydration on the basis of symbolic value alone is not very convincing. Most individuals and commissions discussing the issue are more persuaded that artificial nutrition and hydration—automatically provided through tubes with little if any personal interaction between patient and caregiver—do not effectively preserve for most people the symbolic value of giving a cup of water and piece of bread to one in need. They see enough diversity of perspective even among committed Christians to argue for freedom of judgment on the part of those making a particular treatment decision. The challenge for us all is to maintain an uncompromising respect for human life as created in the image of God. We must not withhold artificial nutrition and fluids for the purpose of ending a human life. Some will continue artificial nutrition and hydration no matter what the situation, imminent death or not. Others will recognize that there are occasions when these interventions can lose their benefit and perhaps do harm. Under such circumstances they may cease them, not out of disrespect but as an expression of faith that sees beyond perseverance and death into the hope for which we have longed (Rom. 5:1–5; 8:20–24).

23. *Should my desire to be with Christ in eternity play a part in end-of-life decisions?*

According to God's plan, each person will die and then proceed to judgment (Heb. 9:27). The judgment of believers will take place before the Son of God where they will be paid back for their deeds in the body, according to what they have done, whether good or bad (2 Cor. 5:9–10). Just prior to discussing this future judgment, the apostle Paul describes his present experience in light of a future hope that motivates him to live each day of life in a manner that is pleasing to God. In spite of the persecution (2 Cor. 4:8–10), the death threats (4:11–12), and the suffering that accompanies mortality (4:16; 5:1–4), Paul rejoices in the promise of his own resurrection when his temporal decaying body will be replaced by an eternal body. Though Paul's preference was to be with the Lord (5:8; Phil. 2:21–26), it remained his ambition to honor God by serving others. At the judgment seat, Paul knew he would find his reward for being true to God and a committed witness of the gospel he loved.

We have but one opportunity to live in this mortal body and we, like Paul, must choose to live it as fully as possible until the appointed time of our death (Job 14:5; Eccl. 3:2). Medical technology does not give us as much control over the timing of our death as we may think. God is still sovereign. We have been given life to enjoy (Eccl. 2:24–25; 3:12–13) and also to invest in others as reflections of what the gospel of Jesus Christ has done in us. Each breath we take must be taken with the hope of bringing honor to God. As long as we are conscious, we can actively influence others. Though we may desire to be with Christ, never again in eternity will we be able to witness to the lost with our words and lives as we do today. Faithful service to God should be a motivation that propels us through life. Our motivation for service to God on earth is an expression of a love for God that has its root in the hope of eternal life and reward.

As your medical condition becomes irreversible and death draws near, your desire to be with Christ will become stronger as your ability to be a witness to others lessens. Let go of this mortal body and do not look back. Let the disease or injury that has debilitated you walk you into the arms of a God and Savior who longs to clothe you in the garments of righteousness. Serve the Lord faithfully until your time arrives—and through whatever the dying process holds, know that He is waiting to embrace you at the door of your eternal home.

24. Should suffering be avoided at all costs?

Suffering is a broad and mysterious experience that touches all aspects of who we are. It can involve the prolonged physical pain attached to illness and injury as well as the unrelenting anguish that accompanies mental, emotional, and spiritual conflict. Suffering is not something that we look for or desire, or at least we shouldn't. It does seem to find us, however. Our problem is that we tend to view suffering as an absolute evil, a foe that should be avoided at all costs. We are like the young man who, in his immaturity, avoids discussing difficult relationship issues with his girlfriend because he views them as "not fun." His avoidance of an unpleasantness will eventually bring greater disappointment when the girlfriend wisely leaves. Because we live in an imperfect world, things break, plans get adjusted, and people get sick and die. Suffering is unavoidable, but it is not the worst evil.

Suffering is a reminder to us that something is not right physically, mentally, emotionally, or spiritually. It forces us to depend on others, to repair relationships, and to seek answers. Awkwardly enough, this uncomfortable and unsought intruder is a teacher and a motivator that keeps us from slipping into an immature, selfish, and isolated existence. When we structure our lives to avoid all suffering or fail to respond to it appropriately, we create greater suffering, even the worse kind of suffering: people turning against one another in all forms of abuse. In an attempt to prevent our own suffering, we hurt and destroy others through slander, betrayal, and ultimately, through war. Inappropriate responses to difficult circumstances are destructive to life. The solution to suffering is found not in killing oneself or one another but rather in decisions that promote some dimension of healing, in decisions that honor life. It is in this context that palliative or comfort care, during the end-of-life experience, becomes the treatment plan of choice.

The greatest value that comes from suffering is that it reminds us of our need to depend on the Lord. If we ignore God's purpose, we, like Job's counselors, escalate our own suffering and the suffering of others. If we reject the existence of God, we deprive ourselves of comfort in the midst of our suffering and of insights as to the cause of our suffering. We cut ourselves off from the only one who can save us from the eternal suffering we deserve for our sinful self-centeredness. *Suffering asks us to identify its source and then find the appropriate remedy.* We don't look for or avoid suffering; we attempt to respond to it in ways that respect the living and dying experience. Our commitment to endure, to work through and learn from suffering makes our lives, our friendships, our marriages and our efforts more meaningful and lasting.

"[Suffering] is a burying of the soul in the ground, where it waits in the cold, lonely darkness, silent, solitary, waiting for the coming of spring, the warmth of the sun, and the companionship of all living things. 'Except a grain of wheat fall to the ground and die, it cannot bear fruit . . .' [Suffering] is not only the dark soil into which the grain falls but also the soil out of which grows the fruit."[43]

Remember that, as a believer, the suffering you endure at the end of your life is followed by an eternal springtime of warmth and companionship.

25. How does my knowledge of Jesus' last days affect the way I view my own last days?

Jesus did not look forward to the dying process. In fact, the manner of His death caused Him much grief. Knowing that His death was at hand, He took three of His friends to a place where they could pray for Him while He spent time alone agonizing over His coming death with His heavenly Father. During this time, He asked God to remove the impending suffering, but was careful to desire only the will of God (Matt. 26:36–46). We, too, can request the postponement of death and, like Hezekiah, we may receive an extension to our lives (Isa. 38–39). Hopefully, we would not waste this opportunity as Hezekiah did, but remain faithful to representing God in the way we live our lives. But, as with Jesus, an extension to our lives may not be what God wants for us. Nevertheless, we do not have to look forward to the dying process. Jesus' attitude toward it should convince any skeptic that death is not natural but an intruder (see question 1).

Jesus endured the dying process. Once Jesus realized that his death was at hand, He faced each disgrace and indignity as a person whose faith and dependence rested solely in the hands of God, His Father. From the time Jesus left the Garden of Gethsemane, He knew that His fate was irreversible. The indignity that came to Jesus in the form of lies, betrayal, and nakedness may come to us in the form of weakness, incontinence, and isolation. He confronted each indignity, never once denying the inevitability of His death or requesting that a soldier "do Him in quickly" to eliminate the suffering. We, too, will suffer indignities, hopefully fewer with the support of our families, but suffering an indignity does not diminish the dignity of the one who suffers. Jesus was always the Son of God. The nakedness He suffered on the cross could not lesson His personhood or make Him any less important in the major scheme of things. The same is true for us.

Jesus remembered the purpose of His life. Throughout the last day of His life, Jesus was placed before the religious and political leaders of His day as well as before soldiers, crowds, and family. With each confrontation or occasion, He remained faithful to His mission, knowing that He was accomplishing the will of God throughout His life-ending ordeal. Otherwise, as He says in Matthew 26:54: "How then [would] the Scriptures be fulfilled that it must happen in this way?" Do not allow physical deterioration to devalue the last moments of your life. You may not be able to address the highest officials of the land during your dying process, but you will be in the presence of medical personnel, friends, and family members. As long as you are conscious, you actively represent the King of Kings. Be faithful—"For I am confident of this very thing, that He who began a good work in you will perfect it until the day of Jesus Christ" (Phil. 1:6), which, for most of us, will take place *after* our deaths. As long as He is working in us, we can be working for Him! Remembering all the faithful who have gone before us, "let us run with endurance the race that is set before us, fixing our eyes on Jesus, the author and perfecter of faith, who for the joy set before Him endured the cross, despising the shame, and has sat down at the right hand of the throne of God" (Heb. 12:1b–2).

Jesus had a certainty about his future. Before His death, Jesus made it clear to His disciples that He was going to a place from which He would return for them (John 14:1–4). During His prayer to His Father on behalf of His disciples, Jesus said, "I have brought you glory on earth by completing the work you gave me to do. And now, Father, glorify me in your presence with the glory I had with you before the world began" (John 17:4–5). The Lord knew where He had come from, what He was supposed to do on earth, and where He would ultimately end up. Like Christ, Christians have a certainty of a future beyond the grave—the assurance of eternal life.

26. Should I ask God to relieve my suffering?

In the previous question, we addressed this issue from the perspective of Jesus in the Garden of Gethsemane. In his letter to the Corinthians, Paul refers to a physical malady that he called a "thorn in the flesh" (2 Cor. 12:7). Three times Paul prayed that the Lord would remove the malady, but God refused, stating that in his weakness, Paul would find God's grace sufficient. Only in our humility (weakness) do we see the true power of God. If God intervened to limit the consequences of a sinful humanity by making each of us physically healthy and intellectually brilliant, we would have less need and therefore less ability to marvel at the power of our God. And isn't this exactly what human progress and technology has done—diminish our need and willingness to seek after Him and acknowledge Him? Our self-centered spiritual condition makes it necessary that suffering not be completely eliminated for the asking; however, God promises to provide the strength and grace to endure the difficulty. In fact, it is impossible for us to grow spiritually, emotionally, physically, or intellectually without admitting weakness. To ignore weakness is to let it flourish; to recognize it is to understand our need for help. In the acknowledgment of our weakness, we discover the power of God, which will ultimately shape us into the image of His Son.

In the examples of Jesus and Paul, we see requests to eliminate suffering denied so that the perfect will of God could be accomplished. Elsewhere in Scripture, there are numerous examples of people who requested the alleviation of suffering or healing and received it. Hannah wanted her womb to be fertile (1 Sam. 1:9–11); Naaman wanted relief from his leprosy (2 Kings 5:1–14); the Roman centurion wanted his dying servant healed (Matt. 8:5–7); and Jairus, the father of a young daughter who was in an irreversible dying process, begged Jesus for her life (Mark 5:21–23). Each of these requests was honored, and those in need were restored to full health. In all these examples, whether health was restored or not, the result was in accordance with the purposes of the Lord, not with the desire of the petitioner. Each result brought the requesting person into a proper relationship with the Creator and best enhanced his or her opportunity to be a blessing to others. So, if you request relief from suffering, know that the answer to your prayer is for your good and for the glory of God. When God does not remove your trial (yet), that is as much an answer as would be a miraculous healing.

Although much illness and premature death is a product of our living in a fallen world, Scripture also links physical, emotional, and spiritual health to obedience. The way in which we live our lives has much to do with the condition of our overall health.

My son, Give attention to my words;
Incline your ear to my sayings.
Do not let them depart from your sight;
Keep them in the midst of your heart.
For they are life to those who find them,
And health to all their whole body.
(Prov. 4:20–22)

Although God will always forgive us for the poor judgments we make, often the suffering that we experience is the consequence of these judgments. Moses' and Aaron's early deaths are examples of consequences that could not be altered by prayer (Num. 20:11–12, 23–29). Ultimately, it is an expression of the Father's wise love for His children that He grants all people the freedom to make choices and to experience their consequences.

27. How can I cope with the suffering God doesn't relieve?

Some say that anger is a proper expression toward God when relief from suffering is not experienced. Though it is tempting to accept this advice—especially when under the duress of intense suffering—we should not. Trust in God is inconsistent with anger at God. If we are in fact angry with God, it is generally appropriate to express it privately with a close friend or counselor rather than denying it. In this way we can recognize it and the lack of trust it signifies. Through reflection, we will sometimes discover that our suffering is a product of our own improper attitudes and expectations, or that it is a product of living in a fallen world. Suffering can come as discipline to shape us, as a consequence of our own poor judgments, as oppression from those who have forsaken truth, or for no other reason than that we are human— we get sick and die. Any reaction that would cause us to question the goodness of God is one that we must overcome.

When Jesus was being tempted by Satan to depend on Himself, though extremely hungry and weary, He responded: (1) "Man does not live on bread alone, but on every word that comes from the mouth of God;" (2) "Do not put the Lord your God to the test;" and (3) "Worship the Lord your God, and serve him only" (Matt. 4:4, 7, 10). He knew that His Father would not ultimately abandon Him no matter how severe the suffering, even if the end was death.

After her oxen and camels were stolen, her servants and sheep slaughtered, her sons and daughters killed, and her husband stricken with a horrible skin disease, Job's wife, deeply grieved because of her intense suffering and loss, became angry at God. Turning to her husband, who was himself enduring indescribable discomfort (read Job 3:20–26), she asked, "Do you still hold fast your integrity?" and then demanded that Job "Curse God and die" (Job 2:9). Job's wife was not interested in understanding the suffering. Her faith was only as strong as the comforts of her life. Job, to the contrary, while perplexed by his pain, loved, feared, and trusted God.

Although he became distraught and questioned the

reason for his birth, there is one thing that Job would *never* do—curse God. In response to his wife, he said, "You speak as one of the foolish women speaks. Shall we indeed accept good from God and not accept adversity?" (Job 2:10). In the end, Job's faith was strengthened and his *trust* in God deepened. Throughout life, we can never learn so much, or assume that we know God so well, that we can become lazy in our faith. This blameless and upright man went through some of life's most difficult trials to discover that he could love his God all the more. The same is true of us.

Look for the daily graces of God that help you endure your suffering. If the grace of God is sufficient for us, we certainly will be able to identify it. Graces come in many forms, but we miss them because we generally expect more than we need. Graces come to us *through* or *during* suffering—seldom is the grace of God manifested in the removal of suffering altogether, though eventually its alleviation is an experience of His grace. Daily graces can include the soothing touch of a caregiver when pain seems unbearable, a medication that brings peace, a phone call from a friend that breaks a period of deafening silence, a distraction that alters destructive thoughts, sleep after intense bouts with restlessness, the recollection of a song or a Scripture verse that reminds us of God's faithfulness, and death when our journey on earth is complete.

The graces of God can come to both the righteous and unrighteous alike, whether we deserve them or not. The shame is that we seldom notice them. We are so busy looking for the work of His hands that we miss the work of His fingers. Whenever we suffer,

He is there. Don't let your suffering blind you to the Presence that surrounds you!

> Where can I go from your Spirit?
> Where can I flee from your presence?
> If I go up to the heavens, you are there;
> if I make my bed in the depths, you are there.
> If I rise on the wings of the dawn,
> if I settle on the far side of the sea,
> even there your hand will guide me,
> your right hand will hold me fast.
> If I say, "Surely the darkness will hide me
> and the light become night around me,"
> even the darkness will not be dark to you;
> the night will shine like the day,
> for darkness is as light to you. (Ps. 139:7–12)

28. Do physicians have the means available to control physical pain adequately?

Although 25–30 percent of patients who are dying from cancer have excruciating pain, Dr. Matthew Conolly reminds us that "it is not that we lack the means of alleviating suffering, but that, as individuals [physicians], we lack either the knowledge or the courage to properly use the tools available to us."[44] An examination of these matters in the *Journal of the American Medical Association* adds: "The support that might be made available [to relieve pain] is fragmented and unfocused. No one dying needs to be in pain, we know how to relieve pain; in fact, we know how to relieve most symptoms. We know a lot about how to support families and people at the end of life, but none of these good ends are regularly achieved."[45]

Pain is often undertreated because physicians use

the wrong drug or do not provide the proper dosage. Some physicians are concerned that prolonged use of a drug in large doses will cause addiction. However, in three recent studies involving nearly 25,000 cancer patients, only seven became addicted to narcotics they took for relieving pain.[46] In cases where a patient is irreversibly dying relatively soon, addiction seems hardly to be a matter of concern. Worries about addiction or diminished alertness should enter into treatment decisions only if they are the patient's own worries. It is encouraging that schools such as the University of Southern California are now offering a course in pain management. Some even foresee the day when palliative care, including pain control, will become a separate medical specialty.[47]

Pain control is available to provide comfort through the dying process. Let your physician know how you are feeling. If you are in discomfort, don't assume that everything has been done to bring relief. Sometimes the solution is found in an adjustment of the dosage you are receiving; at other times, a change of drug may be necessary. If you are, or can be placed on intravenous pain medication, you may even be allowed to control the rate or frequency with which you receive pain medication. It is good to relieve pain, since pain can significantly limit your ability to relate well with others.

29. What is hospice, and what can it do for me or my loved one?

Hospice is an approach to end-of-life care in which the focus shifts from sustaining life to helping people die well. It primarily involves palliative (i.e., comfort) care and respect care (see question 3) provided by care teams either in a person's home or in a hospital or other institutional settings. Many hospice care teams are vivid examples of those whom Christ said will be blessed in the kingdom of God because they have provided a service to God Himself by serving people whom God loves so much in their time of greatest need. "For I was hungry, and you gave Me something to eat; I was thirsty, and you gave Me drink; I was a stranger, and you invited Me in; naked, and you clothed Me; I was sick, and you visited Me" (Mt. 25:35–36). Hospice care is the last bastion of earthly life that provides holistic personal and professional protection not just of one's dignity but of one's integrity as well. Hospice literally defends the significance of each human being who enters the terminal phase of the dying process by making it possible for that person to sustain interpersonal relationships, spirituality, and a sense of self to the point of death.[48] The hospice care team comes alongside family and friends to represent the terminally ill person as an advocate and friend.

Hospice care teams are usually designed to consist of primary-care physicians, nurses, social workers, chaplains, and numerous volunteers, though physicians are not always actively involved. These interdisciplinary team members use their skills to ensure that the needs of the *whole person* are met: physical, spiritual, and emotional. They are committed to fostering the *best interests* of the patient and the patient's family.

Studies have shown that some physicians, due to the curative nature of their education or training, are uncomfortable with supportive care alone for the terminally ill. They tend to overtreat their patients to be sure they have done all they can—often for fear of a lawsuit or because of a natural inclination to view the death of their patients as a failure.[49] With the present emphasis on end-of-life care, this trend is gradually changing, and there are reports that physicians are more likely to become actively involved in hospice care, especially as they come to accept the fact that palliative care for the dying is a legitimate and necessary medical practice. Know your physician's view of hospice care and what role he or she will be willing to play. If your physician is negative toward hospice care, determine why. If the physician's reasons are not satisfactory to you, request another physician. This is important because terminally ill patients typically *cannot enter a hospice* program without a physician's order.

Hospice nurses monitor the patient's physical condition while also paying close attention to emotional mood swings and spiritual concerns. Basically, they manage the complete care of the terminally ill patient. Nurses carry out physicians' palliative-care orders, which typically involves administering proper medication. Most pain medication is administered through patches that stick to the skin and liquid that is taken by mouth. Though injections and intravenous applications are used, less emphasis is placed on them because they are more discomforting and limit mobility. Nurses also teach the patient and/or family to help administer some medications, thereby helping the patient and family gain some control over the situation. Certified nursing assistants (CNAs) ensure that the patient's basic human needs, such as hygiene and creature comforts, are met.

Other members of the hospice team—social

workers, chaplains, and volunteers—play a critical role in meeting the patient's and the family's broad range of needs. Social workers help the patient cope with the emotional stresses that accompany the process of dying. Many people have difficulty facing the fact that they are going to die; therefore, many want to avoid hospice care because it is an admission that their death is certain and imminent. Social workers in the hospice program help patients who enter the program live with the reality of their impending death. Chaplains join the team to offer their support by providing theological instruction and counsel, reading Scripture, praying, and listening. Volunteers do the practical things that help keep patients purposeful and growing intellectually: reading to patients; going on trips with them to visit special places; providing companionship through conversation or watching a TV program with them; going shopping with them or maybe helping them pick out a present for their spouses' birthday or anniversary, or just for the fun of it. The job of volunteers is limited only by their imagination. Volunteers bring enjoyment and direction into what, without them, would be a boringly technical and futile phase of life. They help us live until we die.

The hospice approach reminds us that suffering "is a complex issue with mental, social, and spiritual components as well as a physical one. If we ignore these other components, then no matter what we do about merely physical pain, the patient's suffering will not be relieved."[50] Hospice provides a diverse staff to help patients freely express their concerns and fears so that they can realistically and honestly face the dying process and death with as little suffering as possible. Love, a caring touch, and proper medication alleviate the vast majority of pain connected with the dying process.[51] With hospice, dying is not extraordinarily prolonged or impersonal. "Hospice represents the highest quality of life for the final days of life."[52]

Both volunteer and federally certified and funded hospices exist.[53] Although volunteer hospices generally do not provide nursing care, medication, or medical equipment (a few do), they are an excellent starting point for terminally ill patients who are still rather mobile and who do not require regular nursing care. However, after their diseases progress, entry into a federally certified and funded hospice is recommended. For a patient to receive federal dollars from Medicare and enter the program, a physician must declare that the patient is terminally ill and is not likely to survive longer than six months. Also, the patient must be at least sixty-five years of age.

If the patient is under sixty-five, federal coverage is limited to those who are disabled or unemployed. If you are under sixty-five, and do not qualify for Medicare, you should carry insurance that has a hospice benefit plan. Upon reaching the age of sixty-five, you will become eligible for Medicare; however, a supplement to Medicare may be necessary to maintain the same coverage previously provided by a hospice benefit plan purchased through a private insurance company.[54] Also, before August 1997, patients who withdrew from hospice after 210 days were ineligible for coverage if they wanted to return at a later date.[55] The United States' Balanced Budget Act of 1997 no longer makes this stipulation. A patient can return to hospice under the qualifications listed above at any time and remain as long as care is medically appropriate. Check the current provisions when you or your loved one first qualifies for Medicare hospice coverage.

Medicare pays a fixed amount per day per patient ($90.00 in 1998) to each federally certified hospice care program. The program receives this amount from the time the patient enters the program until the time of death. It is the responsibility of the hospice director to spread these funds wisely throughout the patient's participation in the program. Although it may cost an average of $30.00 a day for the first month or so, it may cost $300.00 a day during the last few days until death. The fixed daily amount pays for salaries, administration costs, medication, and various kinds of medical equipment. Some hospices receive support through fund raising and donations.

Conclusion

Modern technology has created end-of-life decisions that are excruciating and perplexing. Perhaps in a way, it is good that these decisions are not too easy. To agonize over the withholding or withdrawing of any medical intervention is to maintain a sense of life's dignity and a love for humanity. Should we err, we should err on the side of life and not death.

We know that we must not kill, but we must at some point allow a disease to run its course. Determining when the time is right to let go is often our greatest challenge. Although we are wise to consult the opinions of others, our biblically informed faith, from which the final decision comes, will be judged by no one but God Himself (Rom. 14:10–12).

Pray, hear the counsel of others, and decide. "The faith which you have, have as your own conviction before God. Happy is he who does not condemn himself in what he approves. But he who doubts is condemned" because the decision does not come from one's faith and "whatever is not from faith is sin" (Rom. 14:22–23). Make your decision—God knows your heart.

Recommended Resources

The Center for Bioethics and Human Dignity Resources:

John F. Kilner. *Life on the Line: Ethics, Aging, Ending Patients' Lives, and Allocating Vital Resources.* Grand Rapids: Eerdmans, 1992.

John F. Kilner, Arlene B. Miller, and Edmund D. Pellegrino, eds. *Dignity and Dying: A Christian Appraisal.* Grand Rapids: Eerdmans, 1996.

John F. Kilner. *Forgoing Treatment.* Available in audio and video formats.

Martha Twaddle. *Hospice.* Available in audio and video formats.

Waybright et al. *The Experience of Dying.* Available in audio and video formats.

Other Resources:

Charles Junkerman and David Schiedermayer. *Practical Ethics for Students, Interns, and Residents.* Frederick, Md.: University Publishing, 1994.

Robert Orr, David Biebel, and David Schiedermayer. *More Life and Death Decisions: Help in Making Tough Choices about Care for the Elderly, Euthanasia, and Medical Treatment Options.* Grand Rapids: Baker; Bristol, Tenn.: Christian Medical and Dental Society, 1997.

Endnotes

1. *Random House Webster's College Dictionary,* s.v. "natural."
2. Vigen Guroian, *Life's Living toward Dying* (Grand Rapids: Eerdmans, 1996), 21–25.
3. John F. Kilner, *Life on the Line* (Grand Rapids: Eerdmans, 1992), 131–36, esp. n. 1.
4. Gary L. Thomas, "Deadly Compassion," *Christianity Today,* 16 June 1997, 20–21.
5. For a clear discussion of death as friend or foe, see Dennis P. Hollinger, "A Theology of Death," in *Suicide: A Christian Response, Crucial Considerations for Choosing Life,* ed. Timothy J. Deny and Gary P. Stewart (Grand Rapids: Kregel, 1998), 258–61.
6. Aaron Spital, "Mandated Choice: A Plan to Increase Public Commitment to Organ Donation," *JAMA* 273, no. 6 (1995): 504. See also the 1996 annual report of the U.S. Scientific Registry for Transplant Recipient and the Organ Procurement and Transplantation Network—Transplant Data: 1988–1995, Richmond, Virginia, United Network for Organ Sharing, 1996.
7. H. M. Kauffman et al., "Trends in Organ Donation, Recovery, and Disposition: UNOS Data for 1988–1996," *Transplantation Proceedings* 8 (1997): 3303–4. See also T. J. Cossé, T. M. Weisenberger, and G. J. Taylor, "Walking the Walk: Behavior Shifts to Match Attitude toward Organ Donation—Richmond, Virginia, 1994–1996," *Transplantation Proceedings* 8 (1997): 3248.
8. For an interesting article regarding a plan to motivate individuals to donate organs, see G. Gubernatis, "Soli-

darity Model as Nonmonetary Incentive Could Increase Organ Donation and Justice in Organ Allocation at the Same Time, *Transplantation Proceedings* 8 (1997): 3264–66. He proposes that those who voluntarily choose to donate their organs *prior to the onset of a disease* automatically have a higher priority as organ recipients, should the need arise. He maintains that both justice and the motivation for people to donate organs would be increased through this scheme.

9. L. Roels et al., "A Survey on Attitudes to Organ Donation among Three Generations in a Country with Ten Years of Presumed Consent Legislation," *Transplantation Proceedings* 8 (1997): 3225.

10. The mandatory choice law, if made legal, would demand that each competent adult decide whether they desire to donate or not donate their organs when they die. The answer would be recorded on their driver's license, which they would not receive if they refused to respond to the question. Present studies suggest that a majority of the population favors this law. See Aaron Spital, "Mandated Choice."

11. Charles J. Dougherty, "Our Bodies, Our Families: The Family's Role in Organ Donation," *Second Opinion* (October 1993): 59–67.

12. Cossé, Weisenberger, and Taylor, "Walking the Walk," 3248.

13. Nigel M. de S. Cameron, *The New Medicine: Life and Death after Hippocrates* (Wheaton, Ill.: Crossway Books, 1991), 172.

14. Robert Orr, David Biebel, and David Schiedermayer, *More Life and Death Decisions: Help in Making Tough Choices about Care for the Elderly, Euthanasia, and Medical Treatment Options* (Grand Rapids: Baker; Bristol, Tenn.: Christian Medical and Dental Society, 1997), 75–86.

15. Sissela Bok, "Lies to the Sick and Dying," in *Inter-*

vention and Reflection: Basic Issues in Medical Ethics, 5th ed., ed. Ronald Munson (New York: Wadsworth Publishing, 1996), 295.

16. Charles Junkerman and David Schiedermayer, *Practical Ethics for Students, Interns, and Residents* (Frederick, Md.: University Publishing, 1994), 46–51; John F. Kilner, "Forgoing Treatment," in *Dignity and Dying: A Christian Appraisal,* ed. John F. Kilner, Arlene B. Miller, and Edmund D. Pellegrino (Grand Rapids: Eerdmans, 1996), 12–13.

17. Edward R. Grant and Paul Benjamin Linton, "Relief or Reproach? Euthanasia Rights in the Wake of Measure 16," *Oregon L. Rev.* 74 (1995): 449, 460.

18. Ibid.

19. Ibid., 462.

20. Kristin Davis, "Dealing with Death: A Terminal Illness Can Obliterate the Best-Laid Financial Plans," *Kiplinger's Personal Finance Magazine* (April 1997): 90–95. This article provides many more suggestions for helping manage end-of-life medical expenses.

21. Junkerman and Schiedermayer, *Practical Ethics for Students, Interns, and Residents,* 76–77.

22. Daniel P. Sulmasy and Joanne Lynn, "End-of-Life Care," *JAMA* 277 (1997): 1854.

23. David Orentlicher, "The Illusion of Patient Choice in End-of-Life Decisions," *JAMA* 267, no. 15 (1992): 2101.

24. Howard Brody et al., "Withdrawing Intensive Life-Sustaining Treatment—Recommendations for Compassionate Clinical Management," *JAMA* 336, no. 9 (1997): 652.

25. Choice in Dying, "Legal Developments," 24 January 1998, at http://www.choices.org/legal.htm.

26. The SUPPORT Investigators, "A Controlled Trial to Improve Care for the Seriously Ill Hospitalized Patients: The Study to Understand Prognosis and Preferences for Outcomes and Risks of Treatment (SUPPORT)," *JAMA* 274, no. 20 (1995): 1591.

27. "Final Report of the Netherlands State Commission on Euthanasia: An English Summary," *Bioethics* 1 (1987): 163–74.

28. The SUPPORT Investigators, "A Controlled Trial," 1592.

29. Andrew A. Skolnick, "End-of-Life Care Movement Growing," *JAMA* 278 (1997): 967–69; Charles Marwick, "Geriatricians Want Better End-of-Life Care," *JAMA* 277 (1997): 445–46; and Sulmasy and Lynn, "End-of-Life Care," 1855.

30. Joanne Lynn, "Caring at the End of Our Lives," *JAMA* 335, no. 3 (1996): 202.

31. Brody et al., "Withdrawing Intensive Life-Sustaining Treatment," 656.

32. For further information, contact the American Association of Retired Persons (AARP), Health Advocacy Services, 1909 K Street NW, Washington, D.C. 20049. A helpful guide from AARP is entitled, *The Right Place at the Right Time: A Guide to Long-Term Choices*.

33. James A. Tulsky et al., "See One, Do One, Teach One? House Staff Experience Discussing Do-Not-Resuscitate Orders," *Archives of Internal Medicine* 156 (1996): 1285, 1287.

34. Junkerman and Schiedermayer, *Practical Ethics for Students, Interns, and Residents*, 4.

35. Ibid.

36. Thomas J. Prendergast and John M. Luce, "Increasing Incidence of Withholding and Withdrawal of Life Support from the Critically Ill," *American Journal of Respiratory and Critical Care Medicine* 155 (1997): 16.

37. Brody et al., "Withdrawing Intensive Life-Sustaining Treatment," 652.

38. See George Lea Harper Jr., *Living with Dying: Finding Meaning in Chronic Illness* (Grand Rapids: Eerdmans, 1992). "A central difficulty of living with my illness has been its chronic nature. Unlike some illnesses or conditions, doctors cannot provide a 'cure'

for my lymphoma. What we have been presented is a series of treatments, more or less effective, designed to control or moderate the cancer's growth" (p. 111).

39. John T. Dunlop, "Death and Dying," in *Dignity and Dying,* 39–41. John S. Feinberg suggests the following for someone suffering terribly with a terminal illness: "Do whatever is possible to relieve pain, and do not force the patient to undergo procedures or take medicines already proven ineffective or that have no foreseeable benefit. However, because of the commandment not to take life, do not kill or aid the patient in committing suicide. If painkillers hasten death, but the intent is to relieve pain, giving pain medication is morally acceptable. The principle of double effect applies." "Euthanasia," in *Suicide*, 170.

40. Joni Eareckson Tada, "Decision Making and Dad," in *Suicide,* 475.

41. Choice in Dying, "Issues: Background on the Right to Die," 24 January 1998, at http://www.choices.org. issues.htm.

42. Brody et al., "Withdrawing Intensive Life-Sustaining Treatment," 655.

43. Ken Gire, *Windows of the Soul: Experiencing God in New Ways* (Grand Rapids: Zondervan, 1996), 199. Depression is used in the place of suffering in the original text.

44. Matthew Conolly, "The Management of Cancer Pain," in *Suicide,* 76.

45. Marwick, "Geriatricians," 445.

46. Susan Brink, "Best Hospitals 1997," *U.S. News and World Report,* 28 July 1997, 62.

47. Richard L. Worsnop, "Caring for the Dying," *CQ Researcher,* 5 September 1997, 775.

48. Martha L. Twaddle, "Hospice Care," in *Dignity and Dying,* 184.

49. Brink, "Best Hospitals," 58, reports that "doctors are far less paternalistic today. . . . Yet they are trained to

view death as a failure of medicine and feel compelled to err on the side of doing more rather than less. Grieving families also reinforce the impulse to do whatever is possible, even when treatment has virtually no chance of helping the patient." See also the SUPPORT Investigators, "A Controlled Trial," 1591–92. Worsnop, "Caring for the Dying," 771, states that "although its influence is steadily increasing, the hospice philosophy runs counter to the goals of most American medical practitioners. Their overriding concern is preservation of life, and the death of a patient is often regarded as a personal and professional failure." See also William E. Phipps, *Death: Confronting the Reality* (Atlanta: John Knox Press, 1987), 55.

50. Conolly, "The Management of Cancer Pain," 75.

51. Twaddle, "Hospice Care," 185. See also Phipps, *Death,* 58. Speaking of hospice, Phipps states that "high priority is given to relieving pain, with phenomenal success. A study of English hospices showed that thirty-seven percent of those admitted were experiencing severe pain. All but one percent of them found relief after admission." Note that this remark was made in 1987; pain technology has advanced much further since then.

52. Worsnop, "Caring for the Dying," 777.

53. As of September 1997, 2,154 federally certified hospices were operating "compared with 1,011 in 1991 and only 158 in 1985. "The leading hospice states," according to the Hospice Association, "are California, Georgia, North Carolina, Ohio, Pennsylvania, and Texas." Worsnop, "Caring for the Dying," 782.

54. Some of the preceding material is adapted from an interview with Mary Jo O'Malley, Director of the Condell Home Care and Hospice. 111 W. Church Street, Libertyville, Ill. 60048 (January 23, 1998).

55. Davis, "Dealing with Death," 94.